MEET THE GREATS

Kate
MIDDLETON

TIM COOKE

Gareth Stevens
PUBLISHING

Please visit our website, www.garethstevens.com.
For a free color catalog of all our high-quality books,
call toll free 1-800-542-2595 or fax 1-877-542-2596.

Cataloging-in-Publication Data

Names: Cooke, Tim.
Title: Kate Middleton / Tim Cooke.
Description: New York : Gareth Stevens Publishing, 2020. | Series: Meet the greats | Includes glossary and index.
Identifiers: ISBN 9781538252437 (pbk.) | ISBN 9781538252444 (library bound)
Subjects: LCSH: Catherine, Duchess of Cambridge, 1982---Juvenile literature. | Princesses--Great Britain--
Biography--Juvenile literature.
Classification: LCC DA591.A45 C66 2020 | DDC 941.086'12092 B--dc23

Published in 2020 by
Gareth Stevens Publishing
111 East 14th Street, Suite 349
New York, NY 10003

Contents

Introduction

A young woman meets a prince and marries him to become a duchess. One day, she will be queen of England.

*T*his is not a fairy tale but the true story of Kate Middleton, the Duchess of Cambridge. When she walked down the aisle of Westminster Abbey on April 29, 2011, Kate left behind her old life as a **commoner**. And by the time she left the abbey, Kate was a **duchess**. She was now the wife of Prince William, the Duke of Cambridge. William is the queen's grandson and will become king after his father, Prince Charles.

Born into a wealthy family in England, Kate enjoyed a **privileged** childhood. Her family were businesspeople, however, rather than members of the British **aristocracy**. There was nothing in her early life to suggest that Kate might one day marry one future king and become the mother of another.

A Privileged UPBRINGING

Kate's great-grandfather had worked in a coal mine, but Kate grew up with a comfortable lifestyle in the countryside.

Catherine Elizabeth Middleton was born on January 9, 1982, in Reading, a town in southern England. She was the oldest of Michael and Carole Middleton's three children. Her sister Pippa was born in 1983 and their brother James in 1987. Michael and Carole met when they worked for British Airways. Carole came from a working background, but Michael's **ancestors** were lawyers and landowners. When Kate (as Catherine was usually known) was born, her father still worked for British Airways, but her mom quit to raise her first child.

QUICK FACTS

✤ Kate grew up in a middle-class family. Her mother became a successful businesswoman.

✤ Kate was smart and good at sports, but she was also quite shy and was bullied at school.

Amman in Jordan is a busy city built up around an ancient Roman theater.

AN EXCITING ADVENTURE

In 1984, when Kate was just two years old and Pippa was a baby, British Airways sent Michael to work in Amman, Jordan, in the Middle East. The whole family moved and stayed there until 1986. Kate went to an English-speaking nursery. When she wasn't at school she enjoyed playing in the sun with her baby sister.

When the family returned to England in 1986, they settled in the county of Berkshire. Kate was enrolled in a private school, St. Andrew's. She stayed there until she was 13 years old.

The school was a boarding school. As Kate grew older, she lived at school during the week, but returned home on weekends.

AN ENTERPRISING MOM

Carole had a busy time as mom to three children. The Middleton children were often invited to parties. Carole noticed that the party bags they brought home were often full of gifts the children did not want. She wondered why the bags were not filled with fun things that kids really wanted. That sparked an idea that turned into a very successful business. Starting in the garden shed, Carole built up her Party Pieces business into a multimillion-dollar business.

Party Pieces makes and sells all sorts of gifts for children's parties.

Party Pieces became so successful that Michael left British Airways to help out. The extra money meant that the family could afford to move to a bigger house. When Kate was 13, she left St. Andrew's to attend Downe House. This was a girl's boarding school in the tiny village of Cold Ash in Berkshire.

A DIFFICULT TIME

Kate's time at Downe House was not a happy experience. Kate was hardworking and very sporty, but she was also shy. She had problems fitting in at the school. She later revealed that she had been bullied there.

Kate found it hard to learn lacrosse, which involves catching and throwing the ball with baskets on sticks.

Marlborough College in Wiltshire has about 850 students.

One problem was that she joined at age 13, when most of the girls had arrived at 11. They had already formed their friendship groups, so it was hard for Kate to make friends. Although she was an outstanding field hockey player, Kate had never played the school's main game, lacrosse. After just two terms, she left Downe House for another boarding school.

MARLBOROUGH COLLEGE

Founded in 1843 as a school for the sons of **clergymen**, Marlborough College was a mixed school by the time Kate joined. With its grand buildings and hundreds of acres of playing fields, the college is most people's idea of what a British boarding school looks like.

GOING FORWARD

Kate's five years at Marlborough were very happy. She worked hard, and her grades were good enough for her to be able to go to almost any university. She decided that she would study art history at the University of Edinburgh, in Scotland.

First, she took a gap year between school and university. Gap years can be spent **volunteering**, working, traveling, studying, or a combination of these things. Kate decided to improve her knowledge of art by enrolling in a course in the birthplace of the **Renaissance**, Florence in Italy. She spent 12 weeks in the city.

Florence is home to great masterpieces, like Titian's *Primavera*. Kate also learned some Italian while she was there.

Patagonia is a remote region at the southernmost tip of South America.

TO THE ENDS OF THE EARTH

After studying art in Italy, Kate wanted to do something very different. In January 2001, she volunteered with Operation Raleigh (now known as Raleigh International) in Patagonia, Chile. The **charity** encourages **sustainable development** in remote communities around the world. By chance, Kate's future husband, Prince William, had also spent part of his gap year in Chile.

Kate trekked through the Patagonian wilderness before she worked on a **marine conservation** program, helped build a fire station, and taught English. Along with other volunteers, Kate loved the experience of meeting new people and helping others less fortunate than herself.

Boarding
SCHOOLS

Kate spent much of her education at boarding schools. This type of residential school has a long history in Great Britain.

The earliest boarding schools date from the Middle Ages. They get their name because students got "room and board," meaning they slept and ate all their meals at school. By the 1800s, boarding schools had become the choice of rich or well-connected Britons, who sent their sons away to be educated. At that time most of the schools only accepted boys.

Boarding schools are known for their facilities, such as these science labs at Marlborough College.

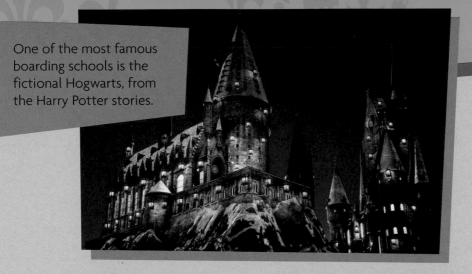

One of the most famous boarding schools is the fictional Hogwarts, from the Harry Potter stories.

Today, most boarding schools in Great Britain are fee-paying schools. Many now admit girls, and there are also girls-only boarding schools like Downe House. They are very expensive, so usually only wealthy families can afford to send their children to a boarding school. Students even come from overseas to be educated.

Traditional boarding schools often have large playing fields, sports centers, theaters, and other facilities that are not found in most normal British schools. Prince William and his brother Harry attended Eton College. It is one of the oldest boys' boarding schools. Eton is known for producing politicians and successful businesspeople.

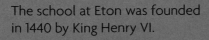
The school at Eton was founded in 1440 by King Henry VI.

Courtship and
MARRIAGE

When Kate decided at the last minute to switch to St. Andrews University, she had no idea how this would affect her life.

Edinburgh had been Kate's first choice, but she changed her mind. St. Andrews has a good **reputation** for art, her chosen subject. She had done well enough in her exams to allow her to make the switch. St. Andrews also appealed to her because of its location. Unlike Edinburgh, which is in Scotland's capital city, St. Andrews is in a quiet coastal town just north of Edinburgh. Kate arrived there in fall 2001. By chance, another of the freshmen arriving at the university at the same time was Prince William, **heir** to the British throne.

QUICK FACTS

❖ Kate met Prince William at university. They become friends before falling in love.

❖ She found the pressure of dating the heir to the throne so difficult that the couple split up for a short time.

St. Andrews is the oldest university in Scotland. It was founded in 1413.

COLLEGE LIFE

Kate and William had both chosen to live in a university hall of residence during their first year. The advantage of living in a hall was that meals were provided. The dining room was a great place to get to know other students. Kate and William were both assigned to St. Salvator's Hall. It housed 147 students in its old block and a more modern **annex**. The students each had their own bedroom, but they had to share bathrooms.

In such a small hall, Kate and William's paths were bound to cross. At first they were both studying art history, although William later switched to major in Geography. They were both sporty and loved being outdoors. The two soon became friends.

A FASHION SHOW

Over Kate's first year, her friendship with the prince even grew closer. Then, in March 2002, Kate offered to model in a charity fashion show. She agreed to wear a knitted lace skirt designed by a friend. She was bound to make the skirt look great. One of the members of the audience was Kate's friend, William. He took notice of her poise and beauty up on the catwalk.

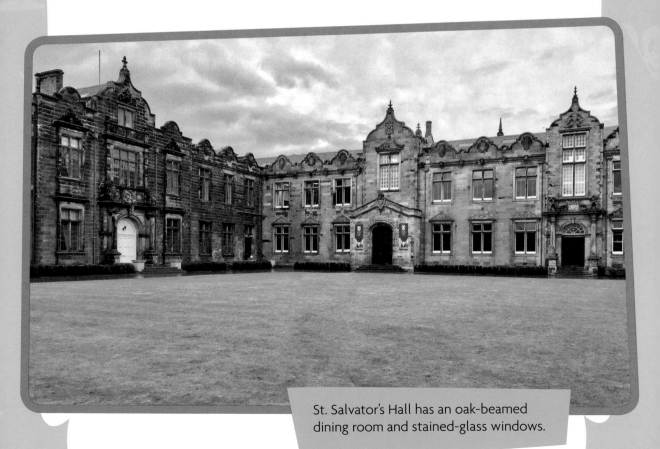

St. Salvator's Hall has an oak-beamed dining room and stained-glass windows.

Prince William was considered one of the most eligible men in the world.

A PRIVATE ROMANCE

In their second year, Kate and William moved out of halls and into a private apartment, which they shared with roommates. Their friendship continued to deepen, and they both went to each other's 21st birthday parties. Sometime in late 2003, the friendship turned to love.

The first sign the world had that Prince William had a girlfriend came in March 2004. He and Kate were photographed skiing together in Klosters, Switzerland. Eager to protect Kate, William denied that she was his girlfriend. He was determined that the press would not chase her as they had pursued his late mother, Princess Diana.

A COUPLE

After the couple graduated university, their relationship carried on in secret. In January 2006, the two were photographed kissing at Klosters. The secret was out.

By now, Prince William was at military academy, training to be an officer. Kate was in a difficult position. Eager to keep her independence, Kate went to work. She got a job as an **accessories** buyer for a fashion store, Jigsaw. Because she was not a member of the royal family, however, she had no protection. Photographers could follow her as much as they wanted to snap a picture, which they could sell for thousands of dollars. Pressures started to mount on the young woman.

Klosters in the Alps is one of the most fashionable ski resorts in Europe.

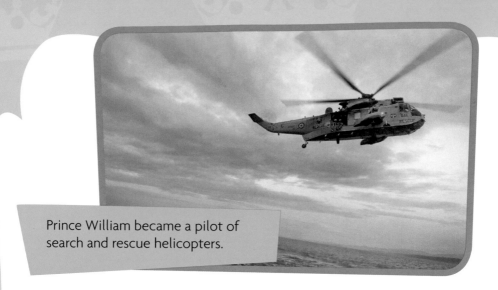

Prince William became a pilot of search and rescue helicopters.

Perhaps as a result of all the press attention, in April 2007 it was confirmed that Kate and William had split up. The split did not last long, however, and the couple reunited in June 2007. It was not until the following April that they were seen together at a formal royal occasion. Kate watched as William received his **wings** as a qualified pilot in the Royal Air Force from his father, the Prince of Wales.

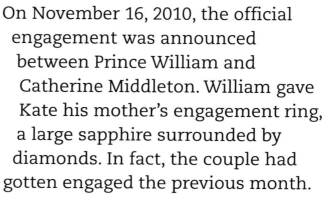

AN ENGAGEMENT

On November 16, 2010, the official engagement was announced between Prince William and Catherine Middleton. William gave Kate his mother's engagement ring, a large sapphire surrounded by diamonds. In fact, the couple had gotten engaged the previous month.

William had proposed to Kate while they were on vacation in Kenya, Africa. By then, the couple were living together. William's job as a helicopter pilot had taken him to the island of Anglesey in a remote part of Wales. There, the couple rented a cottage and lived a normal life away from the cameras and the glare of publicity.

The wedding was to take place in Westminster Abbey on April 29 the next year. Before then, Kate had a lot to do! She had to choose a wedding dress, and decide who would be her bridesmaids and pages. There were many details to organize for a wedding that would be televised across the world.

Only about 70,000 people live on Anglesey, which is joined to the Welsh mainland by a short bridge.

The Royal Family and THE PRESS

William's mother, Princess Diana, died in a car crash in Paris in 1997. William and his brother, Harry, blamed the press for her death.

Princess Diana's beauty and glamor had made her an international superstar after she married Prince Charles in 1981. Everyone wanted to see pictures of Diana, and photographers followed her wherever she went. All senior members of the royal family have their own security guards, but this did not stop photographers from trying to get close to Diana to get a picture.

Members of the royal family are photographed everywhere they go. Their pictures help to sell newspapers.

This tribute edition of a newspaper shows Diana with the young princes William (left) and Harry.

When Diana died, the car she was traveling in was being chased by paparazzi. These are photographers who make money by selling images of celebrities. William and Harry blamed the paparazzi, and their relationship with the press deteriorated.

Because of what happened to their mother, the princes have tried to protect themselves and those closest to them from the **media**. This was difficult when Kate became William's girlfriend. Becoming the girlfriend of a prince meant she had to give up her privacy. However, she still had no official role. At that time, there was no guarantee that the relationship would last.

William (left) and Harry walk with their father and uncle in their mother's funeral procession.

A Royal FAMILY

On April 29, 2011, around 1,900 guests gathered in Westminster Abbey as Kate married Prince William.

*T*housands of people lined London's streets to get a glimpse of the couple as they rode in carriages to and from the abbey. A worldwide audience of around 300 million watched on TV. The wedding went off perfectly. Kate looked stunning in a wedding dress by the British design firm Alexander McQueen. As William met Kate at the altar, he told her how beautiful she looked. And she did. Without any trace of nerves, she repeated her vows. Once she was married, she became a member of the royal family and had her own royal title. Kate Middleton was now the Duchess of Cambridge.

QUICK FACTS

❊ Kate became a member of the royal family when she married William in 2011.

❊ The couple had three children, including Prince George, who will one day be king.

MARRIED LIFE

After a honeymoon in the Seychelles, an island group in the Indian Ocean, it was back to normal life for the new Duchess of Cambridge. She and her husband returned to their cottage on Anglesey. William resumed his job as a search and rescue pilot. William's grandmother, Queen Elizabeth II, had lived on the Mediterranean island of Malta for two years as a newlywed. Her husband Prince Philip was working there as a Royal Navy officer. Kate and William were also determined to have some time together as a young married couple away from the demands of royal duties.

Kate waves to the crowds from an open carriage on her wedding day.

The royal wedding was a huge celebration that catapulted Kate into public life.

Kate looked after their rental home, shopped in the local food store, and enjoyed spending time with her new husband. They both knew that this would be the only period in their lives together when they would not be in the public eye.

A NEW ADDITION

In December 2012, Buckingham Palace announced that Kate was expecting her first child. The announcement was made very early because Kate was suffering from an extreme **morning sickness**. The condition made her so sick she had to go to the hospital. The couple moved to London to be near physicians who could care for her. On July 22, 2013, Kate gave birth to the couple's first child,

With the arrival of Prince George, Kate's life changed again. William gave up his job in Anglesey so the couple could move to London and start their royal duties. They moved to a large apartment in Kensington Palace, in the heart of the capital.

As well as a home in London, the Queen gave William and Kate a house, Anmer Hall, on her estate at Sandringham in eastern England. She wanted the young family to have a home that was completely private. Kate oversaw **renovation** work of the 10-bedroom mansion, which has a swimming pool, tennis court, and large gardens. It is a perfect escape from London for the family.

A number of members of the royal family have apartments inside Kensington Palace.

Kate leaves the hospital with William after the birth of Princess Charlotte in 2015.

THE FAMILY GROWS

On May 2, 2015, Kate gave birth to her second child, a daughter, who was named Princess Charlotte. Her third child, Prince Louis, was born on April 23, 2018. On both occasions, Kate suffered from the same terrible morning sickness that had affected her when she was pregnant with George.

When Prince George was eight months old, the young parents had hired a Spanish nanny, Maria Teresa Turrion Borrallo, to help take care of him. As the family grew, Maria Teresa also helped look after each of the new arrivals. She remains an indispensable part of the family's team because Kate is a working mom.

PUBLIC DUTIES

Since she married William in 2011, Kate has carried out thousands of public engagements both in Great Britain and abroad. Wherever possible, Kate likes her children to accompany her and her husband on foreign trips. In April 2014, when Prince George was almost nine months old, he accompanied his parents on a trip to Australia and New Zealand.

In July 2017, George and Charlotte went with their parents on a short trip to Poland and Germany.

In between greeting important people and carrying out her duties, Kate had to make sure that the young children were not bored.

William and Kate chat to President Barack Obama and his wife, Michelle, in Buckingham Palace in 2011.

Kate (center) appears on the balcony of Buckingham Palace with other members of the royal family.

A HANDS-ON MOM

Kate puts her children above her royal duties. She makes sure that whenever possible she is at home when the two older children get home from school and nursery school. She likes to host playdates for the children's friends and to be around for bath and bedtime. Both she and William want their children to have as normal an upbringing as is possible for an heir to the British throne and his siblings. Kate divides George's school drop-offs with William, enjoying the car ride with her young son whenever she can.

Royal BABIES

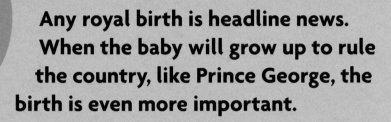

Any royal birth is headline news. When the baby will grow up to rule the country, like Prince George, the birth is even more important.

Royal births are surrounded by tradition. For centuries, for example, the royal father was not at the birth. The only men present were government officials. Their job was to check that the birth took place regularly, so they could confirm that the baby was a genuine royal!

The London Eye is the focus of a red, white, and blue light show to celebrate the birth of Prince George in 2013.

News of the birth of Archie Harrison is displayed in front of Buckingham Palace in 2019.

The first royal male to witness a royal birth was Prince Philip, when the Queen had Prince Edward in 1964. Philip's oldest son, Charles, attended the births of both his sons, William and Harry. Prince William was at the births of all three of his children. Until the late 1970s, royal mothers usually gave birth in Buckingham Palace. Since then, however, most royal births have taken place in a hospital in London. There is a special doctor who delivers royal babies.

The arrival of a royal baby is traditionally made public when a notice is displayed in front of Buckingham Palace. However, the Duke and Duchess of Sussex broke with tradition in 2019. Before the easel was set up at the palace, they announced the arrival of Archie Harrison via their official Instagram account.

Crowds gather outside Buckingham Palace to celebrate the birth of Prince George.

A New Kind of ROYAL

Kate's arrival signaled a new direction for the British royal family. She has tried to make it more relevant to the lives of ordinary people.

Kate has built on the **legacy** of William's mother, Princess Diana. Diana was seen as bringing a breath of fresh air to the royal family. When she died in 1997, however, many people thought the royal family did not share the same sense of loss and tragedy as most of the population. There was a delay, for example, before flags at royal residences were lowered to half-mast as a sign of respect for the dead. This made the family unpopular and out of touch with the modern world. Their reputation has since recovered—and Kate is well placed to help the family remain as popular as it is today.

QUICK FACTS

✣ Kate tries to bring up her children as normally as possible.

✣ She supports charities that work with mental health, troubled children, and the arts.

One of Kate's main interests is helping to stop online bullying.

A FORCE FOR GOOD

From the start, Kate made it clear which areas she most wanted to work in. She wanted to support charities that help children and that deal with mental health issues. Having been bullied at school, she has spoken out about the dangers of bullying, including **cyberbullying**. She has worked hard with different organizations and charities to help children who have been **excluded** from school or are struggling with different emotional issues. By openly talking about the needs of vulnerable children, Kate wants to help those children to feel they can trust grown-ups and can get help when they need it.

HELPING MOMS

As a young mom herself, Kate has also talked about how tough the first few months of motherhood can be on a mom's mental well-being. She works with charities to take away the **stigma** that sometimes goes with talking about mental health issues. She argues that, just as a broken leg needs to be fixed, so mental health issues, such as depression or anxiety, need to be helped. By speaking out about subjects that have been ignored in the past, Kate is helping to break down barriers. If a future queen of England finds being a mom hard at times, then it is no surprise that so many other moms around the world might find it tricky.

Wherever she goes, Kate is handed presents to pass on to her children.

HEADS TOGETHER

Along with Prince William and her brother-in-law, Prince Harry, the Duke of Sussex, Kate created Heads Together. This organization brings together eight leading mental health charities to change the stigma attached to mental health. Meghan Markle, who became the Duchess of Sussex in 2018, joined Heads Together, too. The four royals hope to improve mental health care by raising awareness. In 2017, Heads Together was the lead charity for the London Marathon. This helped raise millions of dollars for its work.

Kate is also **patron** of a number of sports charities. She believes that as many people should play sports as possible. Kate argues that even those who do not play sports can take a walk to help get fit and stay healthy.

Harry, Kate, and William are high-profile campaigners for better mental health.

An avid tennis fan, Kate is a regular in the Royal Box at Wimbledon.

She believes that exercise and a positive outlook on life are closely linked together. One patronage she holds is the All-England Tennis and Croquet Club. This is best known as the venue for the annual Wimbledon Tennis Tournament.

Kate's other great passion is for the visual arts. She is patron of some of London's most important museums, such as the Natural History Museum and the Victoria and Albert Museum. A talented photographer whose photographs of her growing family are frequently published, she is also patron of the National Portrait Gallery in London.

A GREAT HONOR

As Queen Elizabeth II entered her 90s, she started to scale back her royal duties. She relied more on the younger generations of her family to carry out public engagements. In recognition of the contribution Kate has made to the royal family, the Queen gave her the title of Dame Grand Cross of the Royal Victorian Order (GCVO). Kate received the honor on April 29, 2019, her eighth wedding anniversary. It is the highest civilian order the Queen can give. Other women who have received the order include the Queen's daughter, Princess Anne, and one of her daughters-in-law, the Countess of Wessex.

The award confirmed that the Queen thought very highly of Kate. She recognized how much Kate had helped the family in almost a decade since she had married Prince William.

The Grand Cross of the Royal Victorian Order is granted to recognize great personal service to the Queen and the royal family.

Kate has become a favorite with the public for the skill with which she juggles her official duties with being a dedicated mom.

GOING FORWARD

Kate carries out her role with dignity. Always smiling and happy to greet the thousands of people she meets, she is a modern royal. Whether she is representing the Queen overseas or opening a new center for mental health, she brings glamour to the occasion. A dedicated mom, she is giving Prince George and his siblings a normal childhood while also making them aware of the privilege they enjoy. The future of the British monarchy is in safe hands.

Timeline

1982
- Born Catherine Elizabeth on January 9 to Michael and Carole Middleton in Reading, England; she is usually known as Kate.

1983
- Her sister Pippa is born on September 6.

1984
- The family moves to Amman, Jordan.

1986
- The family returns from Jordan in September. Kate starts at St. Andrew's School.

1987
- Kate's brother, James, is born on April 15.

1995
- Attends Downe House School.

1996
- Moves to Marlborough College as a boarder.

2000
- Starts a gap year between school and university. She spends her time in Florence, Italy, and in Patagonia in Chile.

2001
- Becomes a freshman at St. Andrews University, Scotland, where she studies History of Art.

2003
- She and William start dating.

2005
- Graduates with bachelor of arts degree from St. Andrews University.

2006
- Starts work for the fashion chain Jigsaw.

2007
- She and William split up temporarily.

2010
- October: William proposes to Kate while the couple are on vacation in Kenya.

2010	• November 16: Buckingham Palace announces the engagement of Prince William to Kate Middleton.
2011	• April 29: Kate and William marry at Westminster Abbey, London. They are now the Duke and Duchess of Cambridge.
	• Tour the United States and Canada for the first time as a married couple.
	• On October 26, Kate carries out her first solo royal engagement.
2013	• Prince George is born on July 22.
2014	• The family tours New Zealand and Australia.
2015	• Princess Charlotte is born on May 2.
2018	• Prince Louis is born on April 23.
2019	• On April 29, the Queen bestows the highest civilian order, the GCVO, on the Duchess of Cambridge.

KEY PATRONAGES

❀ National Portrait Gallery

❀ Action on Addiction

❀ Place2Be

❀ Heads Together

Glossary

accessories Items that go with an outfit, such as handbags.

ancestors Earlier generations of a family.

annex A new building joined on to an older one.

aristocracy The highest class in society.

charity An organization set up to help people in need.

clergymen religious leaders.

commoner Someone who wasn't born into a royal family.

cyberbullying Bullying that takes place online.

duchess A woman holding a title equivalent to that of a duke.

excluded Barred from going to school, usually for bad discipline.

heir Someone who takes over a position when its holder dies.

legacy Something a person leaves when they die.

marine conservation Work to protect life in the oceans.

media TV, newspapers, and radio that report the news.

morning sickness Nausea that can affect pregnant women.

patron A prominent person who supports a charity.

prestigious Important.

privileged Having advantages over other people.

Renaissance A period of great artistic activity that began in Italy in the 1300s.

renovation The repair and improvement of an old building.

reputation The general belief in someone's value or worth.

stigma Shame or disgrace.

sustainable development Improvements that do not damage the environment.

volunteering Helping a cause without being paid.

wings A badge given to pilots to show they are qualified to fly.

Further Resources

Books

Hunter, Nick. *Catherine, Duchess of Cambridge*. Extraordinary Women. New York: Raintree, 2014.

Savery, Annabel. *William and Kate*. Royal Family. New York City: PowerKids Press, 2019.

Shoup, Kate. *Kate Middleton: From Commoner to Duchess of Cambridge*. Leading Women. New York City: Cavendish Square, 2014.

Timmons, Angie. *Kate Middleton and Prince William*. Power Couples. New York: Rosen Young Adult, 2019.

Websites

Biography.com
www.biography.com/royalty/kate-middleton
A biography of the Duchess of Cambridge with links to videos.

Causes and Charities
www.royal.uk/the-duchess-of-cambridge
Information about the Duchess of Cambridge and the causes and charities she supports.

Prince George
www.royal.uk/prince-george
A biography of Prince George on the official royal family website.

Heads Together
www.headstogether.org.uk
The website for the Heads Together initiative, spearheaded by the Duke and Duchess of Cambridge and the Duke and Duchess of Sussex.

Publisher's note to educators and parents: Our editors have carefully reviewed these websites to ensure that they are suitable for students. Many websites change frequently, however, and we cannot guarantee that a site's future contents will continue to meet our high standards of quality and educational value. Be advised that students should be closely supervised whenever they access the Internet.

Index